RAND McNALLY

The World of

FLAGS

William Crampton

Rand McNally for Kids

Books•Maps•Atlases

ACKNOWLEDGEMENTS

Illustrated by
Jeffrey Burn
Martin Cosby
Stuart Lafford
Janos Marffy
Eric Rowe
Sharon Smith
Neil Winstanley

Picture credits
6 ZEFA; 9 ZEFA; 10 E.T. Archive; 12 The Admirals Original Flag Loft;
14 E.T. Archive; 17 ZEFA; 19 Pictor; 21 ZEFA; 23 Greenpeace/Gleizes;
24 ZEFA; 26 Associated Sports Photography; 28 Nick Buzzard

Flags produced by
Lovell Johns, Oxford, UK., and authenticated by The Flag Research Center,
Winchester, Mass. 01890, USA, and by The Flag Institute, 10 Vicarage Road,
Chester CH2 3HZ

Designed and edited by
Tucker Slingsby

Published by
Rand McNally in 1994
in the U.S.A.

Revised edition 1997

Planned and produced by
Andromeda Oxford Limited
11-15 The Vineyard
Abingdon
Oxon OX14 3PX

ISBN 0-528-83720-6
Printed in Singapore by KHL Printing Co Pte Ltd

CONTENTS

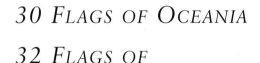

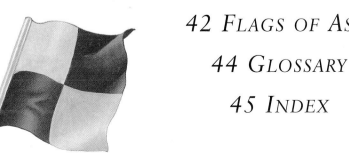

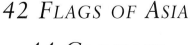

EGYPTIANS
Vexilloids were used by the Egyptians over 3,000 years ago. These vexilloids mostly represented gods but could also stand for provinces or for units of the army.

HANNIBAL
The Carthaginian general Hannibal attacked the Roman Empire and invaded Italy in 217 B.C. with an army that included war elephants. He and his troops adopted and flew flags already in use by Rome's enemies in Italy.

ROMANS
From about 100 B.C. onwards the Romans had an organized system of symbols to identify different parts of their army. An eagle appeared on top of the vexilloid or standard of a legion.

MUSLIMS
Followers of the prophet Muhammad conquered vast areas of land around the Mediterranean from about A.D. 630 onwards. They carried flags, but generally ones without emblems. Their flags did, however, often have words on them, unlike European flags.

ASSYRIANS
The early inhabitants of Iraq, around 750 B.C., carried vexilloids on foot and in their war chariots.

PERSIANS
Over 2,500 years ago warriors of the ancient kingdom of Persia carried standards into battle.

CELTS
The Romans conquered many Celtic peoples in western Europe. These tribes also had vexilloids, often featuring their principal emblem—the boar. Some Celtic standards had a hollow pipe that could be blown like a horn.

FLAGS TODAY

Flags today are made of bright synthetic fabrics designed to be washed and to stand up to all kinds of weather. Until the last century all flags would have been made by hand and embroidered or painted for decoration. Even today a few special flags are individually made by hand.

CRUSADERS
The Christian knights who fought against the Muslims put crosses on their surcoats and shields. As armor developed to cover the whole body and face, so the system called heraldry evolved with each knight having his own device to identify him.

FLAGS THROUGH THE AGES

Flags have existed for over 3,000 years. The earliest flags, called vexilloids, were wooden or metal poles topped with a carving. About 2,000 years ago pieces of fabric were added to some vexilloids for decoration. Over the next 500 years the free-flying fabric part of the flag became more important. A system of identification for knights and nobles, called heraldry, developed around 800 years ago. This led to a great increase in the number of flags. The need for simple signs at sea led to the standardization of national and signal flags around 500 years later. Every country today has its own flag and many groups and organizations have a flag to stand for, or symbolize, their aims.

GENGHIS KHAN
The Mongol leader, Genghis Khan, created a huge empire at the beginning of the 13th century. He and his troops used the horse tail as an emblem of their conquests on horseback.

UNITED STATES 1776
The American colonies had no flag of their own until the American Revolution (1775-83). This flag was used in 1776. In 1777 the Stars and Stripes was created.

ITALY 1848
Like many other countries seeking independence, Italy brought out a tricolor (three-colored flag) in 1848, the famous "Year of Revolutions."

FINLAND 1918
World War I gave some nations the chance to seize their independence.

▷AZTEC FLAG
The Aztec Empire flourished in Mexico in the 14th century. Aztec priests carried a type of vexilloid.

CEYLON
Now known by its true name of Sri Lanka, this island became independent in 1948. Its flag at the time of independence was a revival of the flag of the ancient kingdom of Kandy.

INDIA
The upheavals of World War II led to new nations coming into existence. The former British Empire of India was divided in 1947, and the major part became the state of India. India adopted a flag based on the tricolor of the Indian National Congress.

UNITED NATIONS
The United Nations was founded in 1945. Under its blue and white flag countries unite to prevent aggression and keep the peace all over the world.

SLAVS UNITE
1848 was also the year that the peoples of Slovenia, Slovakia, Croatia, Serbia, and many other states then under foreign rule, adopted a white, blue and red tricolor as a rallying point.

PAKISTAN
The Islamic parts of India became Pakistan. Its flag was based on that of the Muslim League with the crescent and star of Islam.

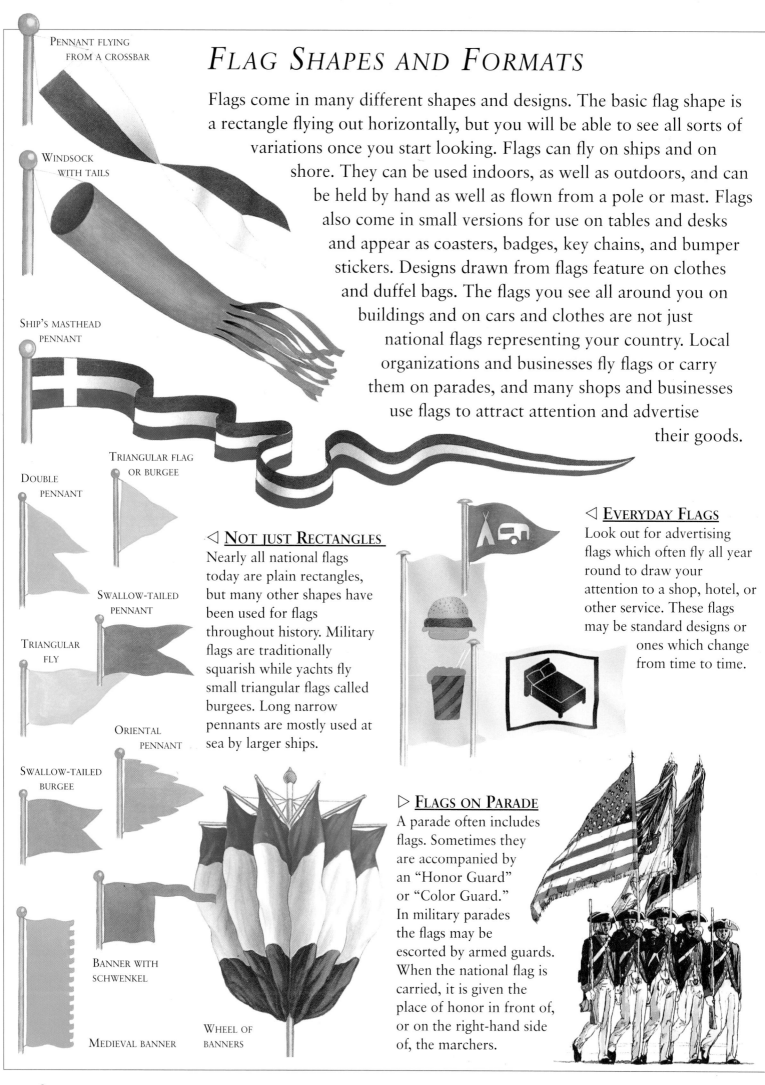

FLAG SHAPES AND FORMATS

Flags come in many different shapes and designs. The basic flag shape is a rectangle flying out horizontally, but you will be able to see all sorts of variations once you start looking. Flags can fly on ships and on shore. They can be used indoors, as well as outdoors, and can be held by hand as well as flown from a pole or mast. Flags also come in small versions for use on tables and desks and appear as coasters, badges, key chains, and bumper stickers. Designs drawn from flags feature on clothes and duffel bags. The flags you see all around you on buildings and on cars and clothes are not just national flags representing your country. Local organizations and businesses fly flags or carry them on parades, and many shops and businesses use flags to attract attention and advertise their goods.

PENNANT FLYING FROM A CROSSBAR

WINDSOCK WITH TAILS

SHIP'S MASTHEAD PENNANT

DOUBLE PENNANT

TRIANGULAR FLAG OR BURGEE

SWALLOW-TAILED PENNANT

TRIANGULAR FLY

ORIENTAL PENNANT

SWALLOW-TAILED BURGEE

BANNER WITH SCHWENKEL

MEDIEVAL BANNER

WHEEL OF BANNERS

◁ NOT JUST RECTANGLES
Nearly all national flags today are plain rectangles, but many other shapes have been used for flags throughout history. Military flags are traditionally squarish while yachts fly small triangular flags called burgees. Long narrow pennants are mostly used at sea by larger ships.

◁ EVERYDAY FLAGS
Look out for advertising flags which often fly all year round to draw your attention to a shop, hotel, or other service. These flags may be standard designs or ones which change from time to time.

▷ FLAGS ON PARADE
A parade often includes flags. Sometimes they are accompanied by an "Honor Guard" or "Color Guard." In military parades the flags may be escorted by armed guards. When the national flag is carried, it is given the place of honor in front of, or on the right-hand side of, the marchers.

PRACTICAL FLAGS

Flags can flash a message to passers-by, so they are ideal for signaling services and information.

BUNTING

T-SHIRTS

DESK FLAGS

DESK BANNER

BADGES

KEY CHAIN

PINS

BUCKLE

FOOD FLAGS

△ FLAGS FOR DECORATION

Some countries have laws to stop their national flag from being used on things such as T-shirts and hats, but many flag designs do appear on clothes, mugs, and bags.

▷ FLAG DESIGN

The same basic patterns are used in many flag designs. A cross, for example, is a very common design on many flags. Also popular are stripes, both horizontal and vertical, while other flags are divided into quarters or given a border.

CANTON

QUARTERLY

TRIANGLE

CROSS

SALTIRE

Cap

Pulley

Fly or flying end of flag sleeve

Upper hoist quarter

Halyard

◁ FLAG RAISING

The flag is fastened to the halyard, which is the rope that runs up to and over the pulley at the top of the pole. One end of the halyard is attached to the top of the flag and the other end to the lower hoist corner. This makes a loop. Pulling on the lower end of the halyard brings the flag up to the top.

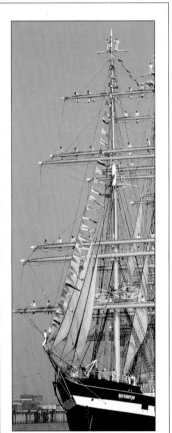

DECORATION AT SEA

For a special occasion a boat may be decorated, or "dressed," with all the flags available on board. For an even more impressive show the crew will "man the yardarms." (See photograph above.)

△ FLAG COLLECTIBLES

Flags feature on many souvenirs. They are an instant reminder of countries and places visited. Mini-flags on your desk or key chain can also tell everyone which sports team you support.

▽ FINIALS

Decorated poles or staves are sometimes used for flags displayed indoors or carried on parade. The top of the pole is finished with a metal ornament called a finial. This could be just a pleasing shape or a symbol of a particular religion or political party.

FLAGS AND HERALDRY

Kings, nobles, and knights usually have their own personal emblem, which is called a coat of arms. The most important part of a coat of arms is the shield that carries a design often reflecting the owner's name or background. In addition, a coat of arms has supporters holding up or standing beside the shield, a crest on top, and, very often, a scroll carrying a motto or saying. Supporters are usually heraldic beasts such as lions or dragons. A system for creating and recording coats of arms, called heraldry, began in medieval Europe. It was very quickly applied to flags, with different colors and images taken from coats of arms being used on heraldic flags

△ HERALDRY AT SEA

An individual with a coat of arms can use it in all sorts of ways. In the past this could include putting it on the sails of a ship.

of all shapes and sizes. A large heraldic banner, displaying the shield from his coat of arms, might be carried by a knight in battle. His troops and servants could be dressed in livery colors—clothes in the main colors used in the design of the knight's coat of arms. Livery colors are so-called because nobles "delivered" clothes in these colors to their retainers once a year.

Schwenkel

Banner of arms

WHO ARE YOU?

This painting of a battle in the 14th century shows what a valuable system heraldry must have been. Flags and clothes carrying identifying coats of arms were essential when knights were covered from head to toe in anonymous armor.

▷ STANDARD-BEARER

The knight's standard-bearer is holding his banner of arms. A heraldic banner is usually square or rectangular and reproduces the color and pattern of the shield of the owner's coat of arms. This knight has two eagles on a yellow background on his shield and the eagles also appear on his banner. Only this particular knight would be able to use this banner. A coat of arms is only granted to one person at a time although it can be inherited or used with alterations by people connected with the owner. His followers had to be content with using his badge and his livery colors.

— *Surcoat*

Canopy

△ HERALDIC FLAGS

Richard III ruled England from 1483 to 1485. He used the royal coat of arms supported by his "boar" emblem. His badge flag had the boar and the white rose of York. This was a simple flag in the livery colors carried by supporters. His standard carried the emblem of his country—the Cross of St. George. A small version (the guidon) was used to "guide" troops.

◁ READY FOR BATTLE

This knight is wearing a surcoat over his armor. His horse is covered by a canopy. Both the surcoat and the canopy are decorated with the shield from his coat of arms. A coat of arms usually has a crest or decoration on top of the shield.

△ NATIONAL HERALDRY

Countries and organizations can also have coats of arms. Some national flags feature a coat of arms. In 1979 the new Republic of Kiribati in the Pacific Ocean chose a winner in its competition to design a flag. The new flag was very closely based on the coat of arms granted in 1937 to a group of islands, called the Gilberts, which are now a part of Kiribati. The flag shows a yellow frigate bird and the sun rising over the Pacific Ocean.

▽ AFRICAN HERALDRY

The southern African country of Swaziland has a coat of arms with a blue shield featuring a real shield and spears on it. The shield is supported by a lion and an elephant. The national flag that Swaziland adopted in 1967 features this shield and spear design. The motto means "We are the Fortress."

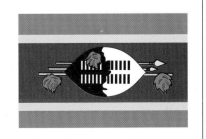

HOW FLAGS ARE MADE

Flags fly in all kinds of weather. They fly in polluted cities and on boats sailing through stormy seas, so outdoor flags need to be made from strong fabrics and attached to flagpoles and masts with firm fastenings. If a lot of copies of the same flag are needed, today's flag manufacturers usually have the pattern printed over and over again onto a long roll of fabric. The printing may be done using a silk-screen process, where paint is dragged across a screen placed over the fabric, or by running the fabric through a printing machine. The long rolls of fabric are then cut up into separate flags. Flags are also made by sewing together different colored pieces of fabric. Large industrial sewing machines are used for big runs, but one flag for a special occasion might still be made on a hand-controlled machine.

△ HANDMADE

Flags such as those used in the French Revolution would have been sewn together by hand. Words or emblems might then have been embroidered or painted on.

EMBROIDERED

APPLIQUÉD

PRINTED

▷ STARS

Stars and other small emblems can be printed on, embroidered, or appliquéd. In appliqué work the star is cut out of a separate piece of cloth and then sewn onto the flag. The flag is then turned over and the material behind the star is cut away so it can be seen on both sides of the flag.

MODERN METHODS

Companies producing flags today use modern machinery and produce any design their customer requires. Even so, much of the work has to be done by hand, just as in earlier times.

▷ FLAG DESIGN

Today's flag designer may choose to work on a computer so he or she can experiment on screen with different colors and devices. The computer can then also be used to plan the making of screens for silk-screen printing, or for controlling automatic sewing machines.

▷ FLAG FASTENINGS

Most flags have a hollow sleeve of cloth down one side. On indoor flagstaffs the pole or stave is just pushed through the sleeve. Flags designed to fly outdoors may have a hoist rope fastened firmly inside the sleeve. This rope can then be attached to the halyard rope on the flagpole with clips or a toggle. An early method of fastening is with loops of fabric, called schwenkel loops, around two sides of the flag. A right-angled rod is pushed through the loops to hold the flag. Quick-release clips may be used at sea. In the U.S., D-rings or grommets are fixed into the sleeve and clipped to the halyard.

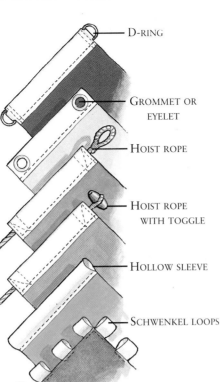

D-RING

GROMMET OR EYELET

HOIST ROPE

HOIST ROPE WITH TOGGLE

HOLLOW SLEEVE

SCHWENKEL LOOPS

▷ MEDIEVAL FASTENING

Early methods of fastening are still sometimes used for modern decorative flags. The schwenkel rail is a rod fixed at right angles to the flagstaff. As well as being fastened on the hoist side, the flag also hangs by its top edge.

△ PRINTING FLAGS

Long rolls of fabric are run through a machine, which prints a pattern over and over again onto the fabric. The printed fabric is then washed and dried before being cut into separate flags. Each flag is hemmed and trimmed by machine and finished with a heading and a fastening system.

▷ CUTTING

In factories where flags are produced on a large scale, fabric is cut using special tools.

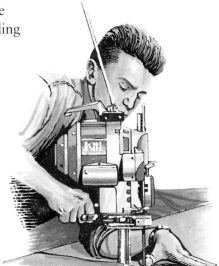

▷ CONQUERED TERRITORY

Raising the flag over a captured enemy position is celebrated in this sculpture which flies a real flag. It shows American marines during World War II.

Imagine the noise and confusion of a battlefield. How can you tell a friend from an enemy? Even today, with all our modern methods of communication, this is not always easy. For centuries, armies and navies have used brightly colored flags to identify themselves. Each time a flag was used in battle it earned more respect, and losing a flag to the enemy was seen as a great disgrace. Captured flags would be displayed in public to humiliate the loser. Sometimes commanders would deliberately put their flag in danger to make their troops rally to the flag and fight harder. Military vehicles and ships still carry simple flags for identification today. Airplanes and tanks usually carry a badge based on the flag of their country.

△ JAPANESE WARRIORS

Japanese warriors, or samurai, had lightweight flags made of silk, which were fastened to their backs on a bamboo pole. This left both hands free for fighting!

BAYEUX TAPESTRY

This 230 ft (70m) embroidery shows the story of the invasion of England by William the Conqueror in 1066. In this scene a Norman is carrying the special flag sent to Duke William by the Pope, as a mark of his approval. The Duke is raising his helmet to show his followers that he is still alive.

△ ROMAN STANDARDS

Each Roman legion had its own standard. This was a decorated vexilloid, which was carried by hand or on horseback. They were often decorated with medals and an eagle on top.

▷ LANCE PENNONS

Pennons (small flags) have been carried on lances by soldiers over the centuries including Norman knights at the Battle of Hastings in 1066 and General Custer's cavalry at the Battle of Little Big Horn in 1876.

▽ CAPTURING THE COLORS

Capturing the enemy's colors gave a great boost to soldiers and could mark the turning point in a battle. Below, a Northern cavalryman fiercely defends his flag from attack by Southern soldiers during the American Civil War in the early 1860s.

△ FLAGS IN FLIGHT

Today's military vehicles and planes often have a badge based on the national flag painted on the side to identify them.

△ MILITARY COLORS

Many military units, or regiments, have their own flags called colors. The names of battles won are sometimes embroidered onto the colors. "Trooping the Color" means parading the regimental flag past the soldiers in the regiment so they recognize it in battle.

▽ THE WHITE FLAG

The white flag is a universal signal for surrender or cease-fire. These flags are never prepared in advance and are usually made out of any materials available. Traditionally, soldiers carrying a white flag are never fired on.

15

△ **COURTESY FLAGS**
Ships and yachts often fly the flag of the country or region they are visiting, as well as their own flag, when entering a foreign port. This is the flag of Normandy, which it would be polite to fly when visiting that part of the French coast.

FLAGS AT SEA

International law demands that every ship today must carry a recognized flag. If a ship hasn't got one, it's a pirate! All merchant ships fly the national flag of the country where they are registered. However, the national flag you will see on a ship is not always exactly the same as the one flown on land. Countries whose flag includes a coat of arms or other complicated design, have simplified flags for easy identification at sea. Many navies also fly a variation of their national flag. As well as national identification flags, ships fly signal flags, company flags, and courtesy flags. Signal flags send messages to other ships, while company flags show to whom the ship belongs. Courtesy flags are flown when visiting a foreign port.

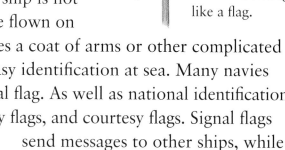

◁ **VIKING FLAG**
The raven flag was flown by Vikings in the 9th century. Some Viking ships also had a metal weather vane that swung like a flag.

△ **HERALDIC TO MODERN**
Flags flown on Spanish ships over the centuries are a good example of how flags at sea have become less complicated. The top flag is heraldic with the royal coat of arms. The middle is a religious flag and the bottom, more modern, design uses traditional Spanish colors.

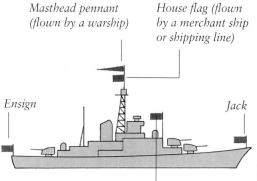

Masthead pennant (flown by a warship)   *House flag (flown by a merchant ship or shipping line)*

Ensign   *Jack*

Flag to signal high-ranking officer on board

△ **JACK OR ENSIGN?**
Flags on a ship have different names according to the position they are flown in. Traditionally, the flag showing nationality that is flown at the stern is the ensign. The jack at the very front, or bow, also indicates to which country the ship belongs.

▷ **IN 1492**
Christopher Columbus used several flags when he set off on his great voyage of discovery. These included the armorial flag of Spain (as it was then) and the personal flag of King Ferdinand and Queen Isabella, his royal patrons.

Look carefully the next time you visit a port and see if you can spot different flags flown in different positions on the ships. On leaving harbor a ship should fly the Blue Peter—a blue flag with a white square in the center. It should fly its national flag too. A ship also makes other signals using flags.

△ JOLLY ROGER

Real pirate flags were usually black, meaning "no quarter" or "no mercy will be shown to those who resist." The symbols of death used by pirates were designed to terrify their victims. Pirate ships had no national flags and claimed to belong to the "republic of the sea." The Skull and Crossbones was only one of many frightening designs used by pirates.

▷ THE ARMADA

Philip II of Spain sent a great fleet called the Armada to fight the English in 1588. The Spanish ships used many flags with different designs. The English ships flew the flag of St. George, which has a white background with a red cross, and the Royal Standard.

△ SQUADRON ENSIGNS

The British Royal Navy used to be divided into three squadrons, the White, the Red and the Blue, each with its own ensign. Then in 1864, the system was abolished and new uses were found for the ensigns. The white is now only used by the navy, the red by merchant ships, and the blue by government ships.

17

FLAGS FOR SIGNALING

Red for danger! Flags can send messages in many different ways. A red flag flying warns you to beware of a rough sea or a hazard ahead. Today's International Code of Signals has a different flag for each number and each letter of the alphabet. With these flags you can spell out whole words and sentences. As well as signaling a letter, some of the flags give a special message when flown on their own. The letter "P" flag is the famous "Blue Peter," meaning "about to set sail." Two letter "P" flags flown together means "keep clear!" The flag for letter "O" means "man overboard." A flag called an answering pennant is hoisted to show a message has been received and understood.

△ CODE OF SIGNALS

The flags running around the edge of these two pages are the flags of the International Code of Signals. Beside each signal flag is the semaphore sign for that letter.

△ SEMAPHORE AND MORSE CODE

Semaphore is a system of signaling with two hand-held flags. The two flags are held in different positions to signal different letters. It is possible to send messages in the dots and dashes of Morse code with just one flag. Hold the flag upright for a dot and sideways for a dash.

▷ HALF-MAST

A flag flying at half-mast shows that something is wrong. Flags are often flown at half-mast to mark someone's death. A half-mast flag is lowered one flag width from the top.

△ DANGER FLAG

In the early days of motoring, a man carrying a red flag had to walk in front of the car to warn people that a dangerous machine was approaching. Red is traditionally the sign for danger, and red flags still warn of road work and other hazards.

▽ OVER THE HORIZON

In the days when all signals at sea were sent by flags, a naval fleet sometimes had a ship on the horizon to repeat the message to other ships out of sight. In this way signals were sent over long distances very quickly.

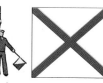

I'M HERE!

Some people have their very own flags. Kings and queens and national leaders often have a personal flag. In Britain, the Royal Standard flies over any building or place where the Queen is present. In the U.S., the Presidential Standard is displayed in the President's office and on his car when he is traveling in it, but it is not flown over the White House.

△ FUN FLAGS

Yacht owners can buy different "fun" flags to send messages, such as "time for coffee" or "large fish caught." They will fly these as well as their national colors and the flag (called a burgee) of their yacht club.

▽ SIGNAL FOR SWIMMERS

When you see a red flag flying on a beach it tells you it is not safe to swim. Look out for other flags beside the sea, telling you if the water is clean and unpolluted.

REVOLUTIONARY FLAGS

A revolution happens when a government or ruler is overthrown, usually by force. The American Revolution started in the 1770s because the Americans did not want to be ruled by the English government. The French Revolution (1789-95) began because many French people felt the king had too much power. During revolutions and demonstrations, flags are a wonderful way of showing support for a cause. A large crowd waving flags symbolizing their aims will help rally more supporters and may make the existing government think again about unpopular policies. Revolutionary groups have, throughout history, attached great importance to creating and using flags which symbolize their desire for change.

EARLY AMERICAN
UNION FLAG

FIRST STARS
AND STRIPES

RATTLESNAKE FLAG

DON'T TREAD ON ME

EL SALVADOR
(1875-1912)

CUBA

PUERTO RICO

GREECE

△ STARS AND STRIPES

When the American colonies were governed by Britain they had no flag of their own. The development of an American flag was very important to the revolutionaries. Their first flag still had a Union Jack in the corner, but this was soon replaced by a design featuring one star for each state. Another flag popular with the revolutionaries was the rattlesnake flag, which had the message "Don't tread on me!" After the success of the American Revolution, other groups and countries created flags based on the Stars and Stripes. These include El Salvador, Puerto Rico, Cuba, and Greece.

◁ THE FRENCH REVOLUTION

The *tricolore* was created during the French Revolution. This far-reaching revolution at the end of the 18th century produced one of the most famous flags in the world. It was used by Napoleon during his conquest of Europe. The blue, white, and red *tricolore* has had an enormous influence in the history of national and revolutionary flags. During the 19th century, tricolor flags began to be used by many other countries including Italy, Germany, Hungary, and Ireland.

26

△ RED AND BLACK

These colors stand for "liberty or death." The Cuban "26 of July Movement" flag commemorates the day in 1963 when the revolution began in Cuba.

ITALY

GERMANY

HUNGARY

IRELAND

FLAGS ON PARADE

This demonstration in Moscow shows how flags add impact and importance to a group protesting or seeking support. At this rally of the Moscow Labor Movement the flags are mostly red to show support for socialist and communist beliefs.

△ THE RED FLAG

The Red Flag has long been a symbol of revolution. The Soviet Union flew a red flag with a hammer and sickle on it. After the Russian Revolution, red flags were adopted by other communist countries including China and the Congo (until 1991). The Congo flag is shown below. Other countries simply added red or yellow stars to their traditional flags to show they supported communist ideals.

◁ RUSSIAN REVOLUTION

One night in October 1917, rallying behind red revolutionary flags, workers and sailors attacked the government buildings and the Winter Palace in St. Petersburg, Russia. Inspired by this, revolutionaries soon took control of other cities and proclaimed a new government.

▽ REVOLUTIONARY CHANGES

The pan-African colors of red, yellow, and green were adopted by Benin in 1959. A communist government came to power in 1974, and a flag with a red star symbolizing revolution was then used. In 1990 a new government brought back the old three-colored flag.

21

INTERNATIONAL FLAGS

Organizations, however large or small, can have flags and use them in much the same way as countries do. Flags communicate without the need for words, and are a good way of uniting peoples who do not speak the same language but who share the same aim. Sometimes the flag of an organization will be specially designed to represent its members, perhaps with a star for each country or state that belongs to the organization. A map of the area covered by the organization is another common feature on an international flag.

△ FLAG FANS' FLAG

Vexillologists (flag students) have their own international flag. It represents the blue sky and the knot which ties the halyard to the flag's hoist rope.

Designing a good flag for an international organization can be even more challenging than designing one for a country. As well as being used as a flag, the design may also appear painted flat on the side of an airplane or truck.

△ NATO

Member countries of the North Atlantic Treaty Organization (NATO) joined together to protect each other. The blue of their flag represents the Atlantic Ocean, and the compass symbol in the middle stands for the direction of all members towards peace.

▽ UN HEADQUARTERS

The best-known international organization is probably the United Nations (UN) which promotes world peace and cooperation. Its flag can be seen on the UN headquarters and also in the many places around the world where UN troops are sent. The UN flag is blue and white, representing peace and tranquillity. The UN building in New York is surrounded by the flags of all member states.

▷ SPACE AGENCIES
The U.S. flag has flown into space painted on the sides of rockets launched by the National Aeronautics and Space Administration (NASA). The rocket at the right was launched by the European Space Agency (ESA). It features the flags of countries that contributed to the cost of the launch.

▽ SYMBOLS AND EMBLEMS
The Organization of African Unity flag (top) symbolizes the wish for unity among African states. The map in the middle represents Africa inside a wreath of laurel. The emblem on the striking flag of the South Pacific Commission (bottom) is in the form of a coral atoll, and the stars represent the member states.

AFRICAN UNITY

SOUTH PACIFIC COMMISSION

△ SCOUTS AND GUIDES
Both these international youth organizations have a "World Flag." These carry the emblems associated with the movements: a fleur-de-lis for the scouts and a trefoil for the guides. Local troop flags are also used.

FLYING A GREEN FLAG

The international environmental group Greenpeace does not have one fixed flag design; different Greenpeace groups have designed different versions. The green background symbolizes concern for the Earth and the dove and the rainbow are taken from the biblical story of Noah's Ark.

▽ RED CROSS AND CRESCENT
The well-known Red Cross and Red Crescent flags are used wherever international rescue work is in progress. The Red Cross flag dates from 1863 and is said to be the Swiss flag in reverse. The Red Crescent was adopted in 1906 for use in Islamic countries.

FLAGS IN SPORTS

Ready, set, go! Racing cars accelerate off the grid as the starting flag is waved. Flags have a place at almost every sporting event. They are used to signal to competitors, to mark the course, to show who has won, and, of course, flags are waved by supporters to encourage their team. Throwing and tossing flags is even a sport in its own right. At an international sporting event like the Olympic Games, where the teams represent their countries, you will see national flags being flown as well as the Olympic flag itself. National flags are carried at the opening and closing ceremonies of the Olympics and the winners' national flags are raised when the medals are awarded.

△ SOCCER SIGNALS
Soccer linesmen carry flags to signal where the ball has gone off the field. These can be in the clubs' colors. Small pennants in the same colors mark the corners of the field.

△ SPEEDING SNOW
A black and yellow checkered flag on a ski slope is an avalanche warning. Snow and ice crashing down the mountain is a real danger to skiers, so the flag should not be ignored.

▷ HIGH-SPEED FLAGS
Racing cars travel at incredibly high speeds, and flags are the best way to send messages to the drivers. The national flag of the host country is often used to start the race, and the checkered flag signals the end of the race. Colored flags are used to pass on other messages.

△ FOOTBALL FLAGS
In the U.S., the teams in the National Football League have flags featuring the team colors and emblems. These follow a standard pattern, but each helmet has a different logo and each flag has a different pattern of stripes.

RACING FOR A FLAG

In Sienna, Italy, teams compete in a horse race for an ancient flag called the Palio. The horses are blessed before the race begins. A colorful pageant precedes the race where banners are tossed and twirled.

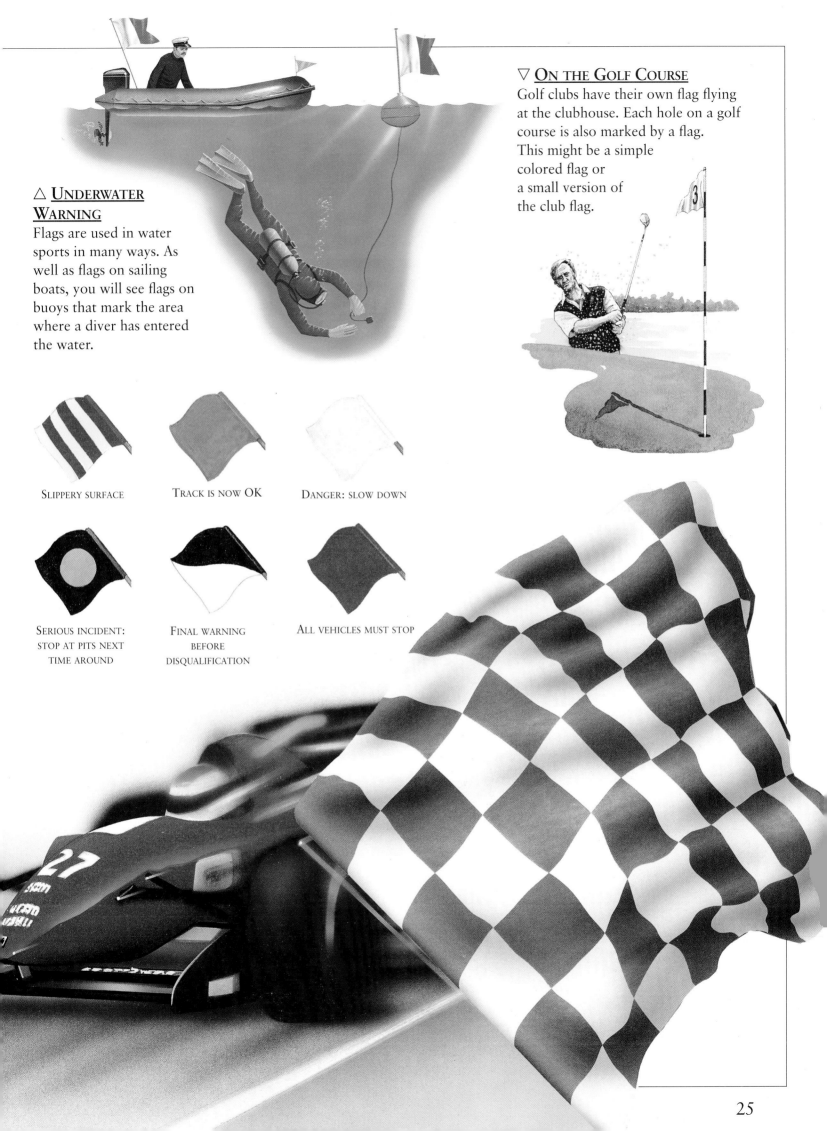

△ UNDERWATER WARNING

Flags are used in water sports in many ways. As well as flags on sailing boats, you will see flags on buoys that mark the area where a diver has entered the water.

▽ ON THE GOLF COURSE

Golf clubs have their own flag flying at the clubhouse. Each hole on a golf course is also marked by a flag. This might be a simple colored flag or a small version of the club flag.

SLIPPERY SURFACE

TRACK IS NOW OK

DANGER: SLOW DOWN

SERIOUS INCIDENT: STOP AT PITS NEXT TIME AROUND

FINAL WARNING BEFORE DISQUALIFICATION

ALL VEHICLES MUST STOP

RECORD-BREAKING FLAGS

How can a flag be a record-breaker? By being the biggest, the highest, or the first to be flown somewhere. When the American astronauts reached the moon in 1969 they raised the Stars and Stripes to remind the world that their landing was a great American achievement. The first explorers to set foot on remote and hard-to-reach places such as the North or South Pole, or the top of Mount Everest, proudly raised the flag of their home country. Displaying a flag which is bigger, or which flies higher, than other flags also emphasizes the importance of a country or organization. Big flags can cause problems though. They are hard to fly, needing very tall, strong flagpoles and a whole team of people to hoist them.

Ingenious ways around this problem include hanging flags from bridges and making a flag into a hot air balloon!

△ BIGGEST FLYING FLAG

The biggest flag that actually flies from a flagpole is the flag of Brazil displayed at the federal capital, Brasilia. This flag is 230 ft by 328 ft (70m by 100m). At this size a flag becomes very heavy and needs a reinforced flagpole to bear its weight.

BIGGEST OLYMPIC FLAG

The Olympic flag flies throughout the Olympic Games. In 1992, at the Barcelona Olympics, a new giant version was also displayed. It was brought into the stadium by a team of athletes and unrolled over their heads. The flag measured 246 ft by 344 ft (75m by 105m) and weighed 1,762 lbs (800kg), even though it was made of very light fabric.

▽ SOUTH POLE

The Norwegian flag was the first to fly at the South Pole. It was raised by Roald Amundsen and his team on December 14, 1911. His rival, Captain Scott, arrived a month later and found the flag still there.

△ NORTH POLE

The first flag to fly at the North Pole was a Stars and Stripes with 46 stars. It was raised on a snow mound by Robert Peary on April 6, 1909. The flag was made by Commander Peary's wife.

▷ TALLEST FLAGPOLE

There is a lot of competition for the title of tallest flagpole, and no one can agree on which is the tallest. One of the main contenders for the title is on the Federal Building in Canberra, Australia. It is 266 ft (81m) tall, but that does not include the height of the building.

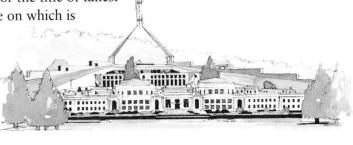

△ FLAG BALLOONS

One way of making sure your flag flies at a record-breaking height is by using it as a hot air balloon. This was done for the Australian flag to celebrate Australia Day in 1985.

▽ HIGHEST FLAG

On May 28, 1953, Edmund Hillary and Sherpa Tensing planted an ice ax on the peak of Mount Everest. Tied to this were the flags of the United Nations, Britain, Nepal, and India. This was the first time the United Nations flag had been honored in this way.

◁ ON THE MOON

A Stars and Stripes was placed on the moon by Buzz Aldrin and Neil Armstrong on July 20, 1969. The flagstaff had a special arm at the top to hold the flag out. There is no wind on the moon so the flag couldn't fly.

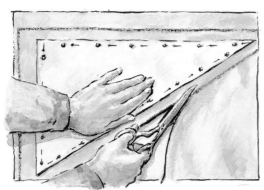

MAKE YOUR OWN FLAG

You can design and make your own flag. Begin by sketching out your ideas. You will need to think about how big and how strong you want your flag to be. A small hand-held flag created for one special occasion can be made from colored or painted paper attached to a stick or cane with tape. A flag that is going to fly out-of-doors will need to be made from strong, light fabric—polyester is ideal. The best way to make a strong flag is to sew pieces of fabric together to make the design. If you are in a hurry, you can make a simple flag from either fabric or paper and make a design on it by using fabric paint or felt-tip pens.

△1. You can make this flag out of paper or fabric. If you are making it out of fabric, begin by making a pattern. Cut out a rectangle of scrap paper about 20 in by 16 in (50cm by 40cm). Cut the paper in half diagonally.

If you are making a paper flag, you do not need to make a pattern—you can move on to step 2.

△2. Pin the triangles to the fabric and mark an extra allowance around the edges as shown on the diagram below. Then cut them out.

For a paper flag, make an allowance for the sleeve on the shortest side of one triangle only: see yellow triangle below.

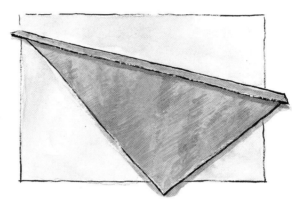

◁3. If you are using fabric, turn in a hem of about ½ in (1cm) along the longest edge of both triangles. It is best to press the hem down with an iron, so ask a grown-up for help.

If you are making a paper flag, skip this step.

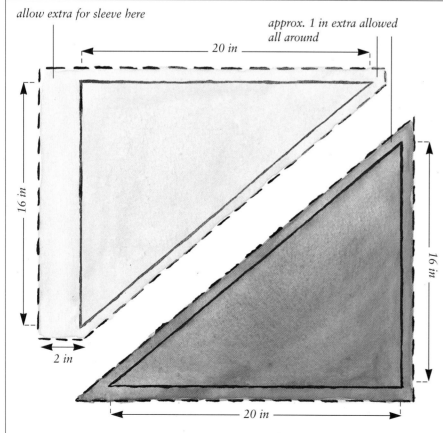

allow extra for sleeve here

approx. 1 in extra allowed all around

20 in

16 in

2 in

16 in

20 in

◁ **DIAGRAM**

This shows what your fabric or paper should look like at the end of step 2. The solid lines mark the position of the scrap paper pattern. The dotted lines mark the extra allowance you need to make for hems and for the sleeve.

approx. 8 in

YOU WILL NEED

- Scrap paper and colored pencils or felt-tip pens to sketch a design
- Newspaper or scrap paper to cut out a pattern
- Pins   • Scissors
- Ruler   • Stick or cane

- **Fabric Flag:** approx. 1 ¾ yd (1.5m) for a one-color flag or two pieces of approx. 30 in (75cm) for a two-color flag plus small piece of white fabric for the soccer emblem
- Needle and thread/sewing machine

- **Paper Flag:** Large pieces of white or colored paper— if you can't get big pieces, tape smaller bits together
- Non-toxic glue
- Tape

- **For decoration:**
- fabric emblems • fabric paint
- felt-tip pens • paints, etc.

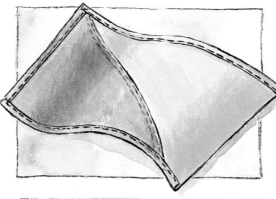

◁5. Sew a hem around three edges of the fabric flag. Leave the edge with the extra seam allowance unhemmed.
Paper flags will not need a hem.

△4. Place the fabric triangles so that the hems on the longest edges overlap. Pin the edges in place. Sew across the overlap twice: once near the edge of the overlap on the front and once near the edge of the overlap on the back. It is best to ask a grown-up to do this for you on a sewing machine because this will make the flag stronger.

A paper flag can be stuck together with tape or glue.

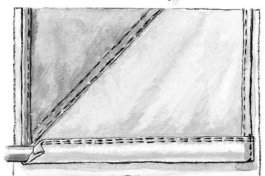

◁6. Sew about a ½ in (1cm) hem on the unhemmed edge. Then fold the seam over again and sew, leaving room for a stick.

Tape or glue a paper flag to make this sleeve.

▽8. To make the soccer ball shape, draw around a plate onto a piece of white fabric or paper and cut out a circle. Use a felt-tip pen to color in the design on both sides—follow the diagram in the box on page 28.

◁7. To fly the fabric flag from a flagpole you need to make the sleeve as in step 6 and then push a piece of rope through it. The rope should be firmly sewn in place. There should be about 8 in (20cm) of rope at either end of the sleeve—enough to tie to the halyard.

▽9. Pin the soccer ball design to the fabric flag and sew around the edge. Turn the flag over and cut away the fabric behind the soccer ball.

If you have made a paper flag, tape your design to one side of the flag, turn the flag over and cut away the paper behind the design.

SOCCER FLAG

This is a photograph of how the flag can look when it is finished. The flag features a soccer emblem and a club badge has also been added. The flag has been made to wave at soccer matches, but you can create any design you like. A flag based on your name would be interesting or one for your school or sports team.

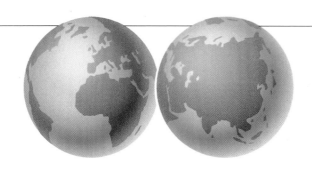

FLAGS OF THE WORLD

Every independent country has a national flag. Often different regions within a country or belonging to a country have a flag. For example, each of the American states has its own flag.

Some countries have one flag that is used on land, at sea, by the government, and by private citizens. Other countries have variations of the national flag for different uses.

Every flag has to look different in some way from all the others; otherwise it will not fulfill its purpose of identifying a particular country or region. However, some countries deliberately choose a national flag that is similar to the flag of another country. This is because they want to show that they have something in common with that country. For example, many countries in Africa use green, red, and yellow in their flag. These colors symbolize the fight to make African countries independent.

On the following pages you can see the national flags flown by every country in the world, together with an explanation of their history and main features. The world has been divided up into seven regions.

Parts of Oceania were once included in the British Empire, and Britain still has connections with some of these countries through their membership of the Commonwealth of Nations. Several flags have a Union Jack on them to show the connection with Britain.

FLAGS OF OCEANIA

Many countries in this region are actually groups of islands. Stars are sometimes used on the region's flags to represent these islands. The layout of the islands may be shown by the pattern of the stars on the flag.

A group of stars called the "Southern Cross" features on several flags. This group of five real stars makes the shape of a cross in the skies above Oceania.

AUSTRALIA
Dating from 1909, it has a Union Jack, a "Commonwealth" star and the five stars of the Southern Cross constellation.

NEW SOUTH WALES

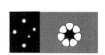

NORTHERN TERRITORY

QUEENSLAND

SOUTH AUSTRALIA

TASMANIA

VICTORIA

WESTERN AUSTRALIA

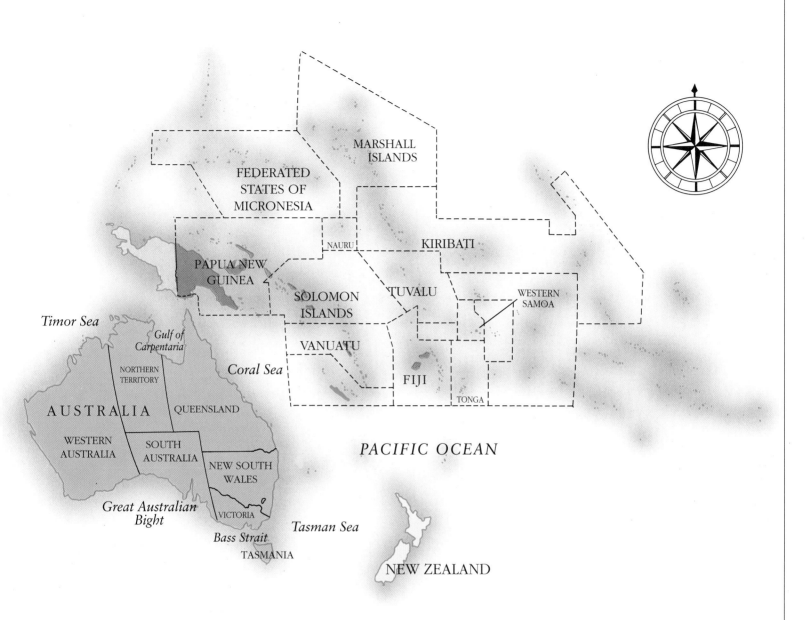

MARSHALL ISLANDS

FEDERATED STATES OF MICRONESIA

NAURU

KIRIBATI

PAPUA NEW GUINEA

SOLOMON ISLANDS

TUVALU

WESTERN SAMOA

VANUATU

FIJI

TONGA

Timor Sea

Gulf of Carpentaria

NORTHERN TERRITORY

Coral Sea

AUSTRALIA

WESTERN AUSTRALIA

SOUTH AUSTRALIA

QUEENSLAND

NEW SOUTH WALES

Great Australian Bight

VICTORIA

Tasman Sea

Bass Strait

TASMANIA

PACIFIC OCEAN

NEW ZEALAND

PAPUA NEW GUINEA
The flag was designed in 1971. It combines the Southern Cross with a bird of paradise.

NEW ZEALAND
In 1869, part of the Southern Cross was added to the British Blue Ensign. This became the official flag in 1902.

SOLOMON ISLANDS
Adopted in 1978. The stars represent the provinces of the country, not the Southern Cross.

FIJI
Fiji is not now a part of the Commonwealth, but it has kept the flag it adopted in 1970.

VANUATU
The 'Y' represents the layout of the islands of Vanuatu. In the triangle are a boar's tusk and two crossed fern leaves.

WESTERN SAMOA
An extra star was added to this version of the Southern Cross in 1949.

TONGA
This version dates from 1864. The cross represents the people's devotion to Christianity.

FEDERATED STATES OF MICRONESIA
This form was adopted in 1978. The stars stand for the states in this group of islands.

KIRIBATI
The Gilbert Islands are now a part of Kiribati. The coat of arms given to the Gilberts was adapted for the flag.

MARSHALL ISLANDS
Dates from 1979 when the islands were under U.S. control. The design was kept after independence in 1990.

TUVALU
A Union Jack indicates membership of the Commonwealth. Stars show the pattern of the islands.

NAURU
Adopted in 1968. It represents Nauru's geographical position just below the equator.

FLAGS OF NORTH AMERICA

North America was once ruled by three countries: Britain, France, and Spain. These countries began to give up their power when the Americans made their Declaration of Independence in 1776.

The original version of the United States flag was adopted in 1777. It featured 13 stripes and 13 stars: one for each of the original 13 states. Additional stars and stripes were added as new states joined the Union. In 1818 it was decided that the number of stripes should be fixed at 13 and a new star only added for each new state. Hawaii and Alaska became states in 1959 and the number of stars on the flag went up to 50.

Canada became self-governing in 1867. The original flag was a British Red Ensign, which is a red flag with a Union Jack in one corner. The famous red and white maple-leaf flag was introduced in 1965. The then prime minister, Lester Pearson, wanted to have a flag that was uniquely Canadian and the maple-leaf design was chosen after much discussion.

Mexico became independent of Spain in 1821. The flag is a copy of the French *tricolore*. It was first used by the army that liberated Mexico from Spain. In 1823 the ancient Aztec sign for the city of Tenochtitlan, which is now the site of Mexico City, was added to the flag.

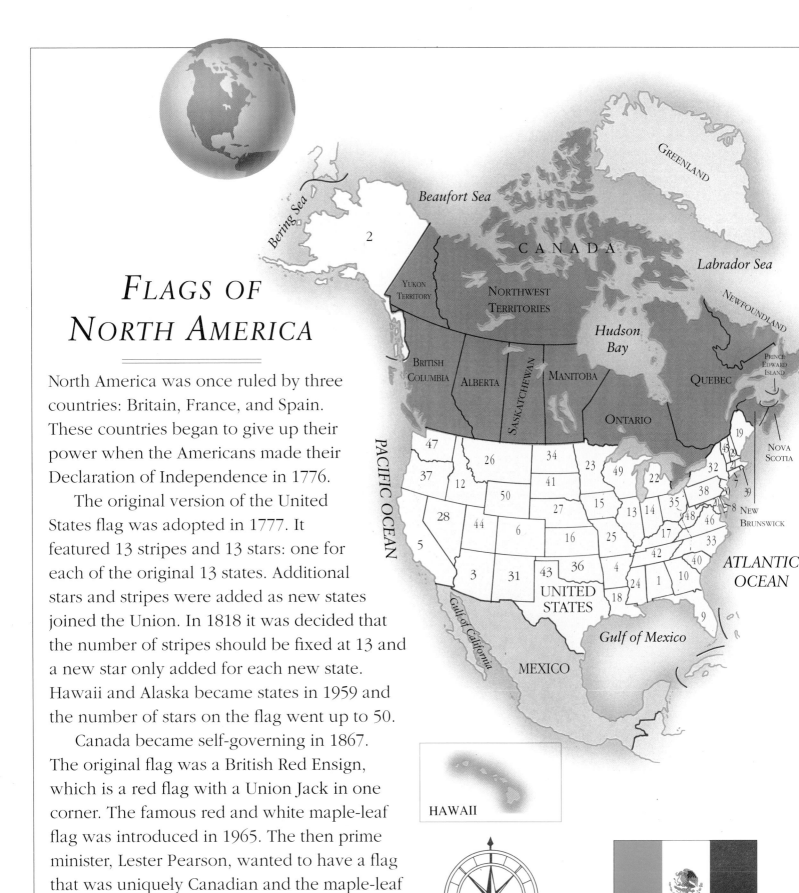

MEXICO

The central emblem is an eagle standing on a cactus on an island and killing a snake. The legend is that the Aztecs were told to build a city where they saw a scene like this. The Aztecs built Tenochtitlan—now Mexico City—in 1325.

UNITED STATES

This flag is known as the Stars and Stripes. The 50 modern states are represented by 50 stars. The 13 stripes represent the 13 original states that existed when the flag was adopted in 1777, the year after the Declaration of Independence.

 1 ALABAMA

 2 ALASKA

 3 ARIZONA

 4 ARKANSAS

 5 CALIFORNIA

 6 COLORADO

 7 CONNECTICUT

 8 DELAWARE

 9 FLORIDA

 10 GEORGIA

 11 HAWAII

 12 IDAHO

 13 ILLINOIS

 14 INDIANA

 15 IOWA

 16 KANSAS

 17 KENTUCKY

 18 LOUISIANA

 19 MAINE

 20 MARYLAND

 21 MASSACHUSETTS

 22 MICHIGAN

 23 MINNESOTA

 24 MISSISSIPPI

 25 MISSOURI

 26 MONTANA

 27 NEBRASKA

 28 NEVADA

 29 NEW HAMPSHIRE

 30 NEW JERSEY

 31 NEW MEXICO

 32 NEW YORK

 33 NORTH CAROLINA

 34 NORTH DAKOTA

 35 OHIO

 36 OKLAHOMA

 37 OREGON

 38 PENNSYLVANIA

 39 RHODE ISLAND

 40 SOUTH CAROLINA

 41 SOUTH DAKOTA

 42 TENNESSEE

 43 TEXAS

 44 UTAH

 45 VERMONT

 46 VIRGINIA

 47 WASHINGTON

 48 WEST VIRGINIA

 49 WISCONSIN

 50 WYOMING

CANADA

The maple leaf design was adopted in 1965. The two red stripes represent the Pacific and Atlantic Oceans. Some people prefer the original Red Ensign flag: the provinces of Ontario and Manitoba use versions of the Red Ensign.

ALBERTA

BRITISH COLUMBIA

MANITOBA

NEW BRUNSWICK

NEWFOUNDLAND

NORTHWEST TERRITORIES

NOVA SCOTIA

ONTARIO

PRINCE EDWARD ISLAND

QUEBEC

SASKATCHEWAN

YUKON TERRITORY

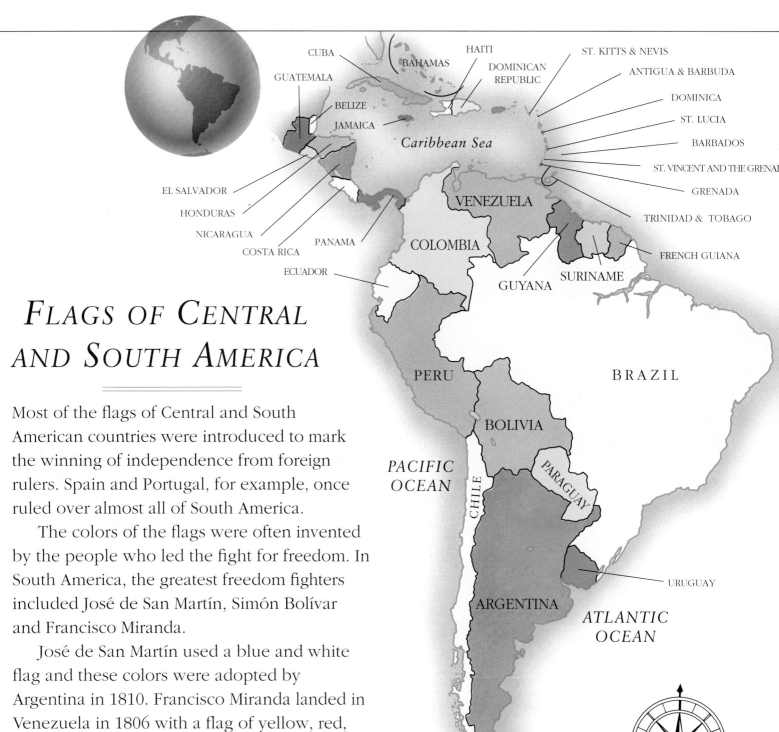

FLAGS OF CENTRAL AND SOUTH AMERICA

Most of the flags of Central and South American countries were introduced to mark the winning of independence from foreign rulers. Spain and Portugal, for example, once ruled over almost all of South America.

The colors of the flags were often invented by the people who led the fight for freedom. In South America, the greatest freedom fighters included José de San Martín, Simón Bolívar and Francisco Miranda.

José de San Martín used a blue and white flag and these colors were adopted by Argentina in 1810. Francisco Miranda landed in Venezuela in 1806 with a flag of yellow, red, and blue. These colors are now used by Venezuela, Colombia, and Ecuador.

In Central America, blue and white were used as the colors of freedom. Five countries—Guatemala, Honduras, Nicaragua, El Salvador, and Costa Rica—formed the Central American Federation (CAF) in 1823. This had a blue and white flag. This federation does not exist any more, but these countries have all kept elements of the original flag.

The emblems and symbols on the flags of South and Central America also mark independence. The "Sun of May" on the flags of Argentina and Uruguay, and the "Star of May" on Paraguay's flag, mark the days in the month of May when independence from Spain was declared by these countries.

Many of the Caribbean islands were colonies of Britain and France. After independence, several islands adopted colors to symbolize their natural resources, such as blue and yellow to stand for their beautiful beaches.

EL SALVADOR
Based on the 1823 Central American Federation (CAF) flag. The national arms are featured in the middle of the flag.

NICARAGUA
Similar to El Salvador's flag, but with the Nicaraguan arms in the middle.

CUBA
Created in 1848. The single star gives it the name *La Estrella Solitaria*.

HONDURAS
Based on the Central American Federation (CAF) flag. Stars represent the five member countries.

GUATEMALA
The Central American Federation flag with Guatemala's national arms. The arms feature a bird called the quetzal.

PANAMA
Adopted in 1903 when Panama became independent from Colombia.

COSTA RICA
Costa Rica is the fifth member of the 1823 federation. A red stripe was added in 1848.

DOMINICAN REPUBLIC
Created in 1844 by adding a cross to the Haitian, flag and putting the colors in opposite corners.

HAITI
Adopted in 1803, this flag was at first based on the French tricolor. The arms appear on a white panel for official use.

BELIZE
Combines the colors of two rival political parties. The national arms are in the middle.

BAHAMAS
Adopted in 1973. Colors symbolize blue seas, golden sands, and the people's strength.

JAMAICA
Designed in 1962, just before independence. The colors stand for hope, natural resources, and hardship.

TRINIDAD & TOBAGO
Adopted in 1962. The colors represent vitality (red), purity (white), and strength (black).

DOMINICA
Dates from 1978. The only flag to include a parrot: the sisserou is a species unique to Dominica.

ST. LUCIA
Revised in 1979. The black, yellow, and white triangle indicates harmony between peoples.

ANTIGUA & BARBUDA
Introduced in 1967, the flag has white sand, blue sea, and a sun rising over a new country.

BARBADOS
Adopted in 1966. Neptune's trident represents the island's dependence on the sea.

ST. VINCENT AND THE GRENADINES
Updated in 1985. The original design, adopted in 1979, featured the national arms on a leaf.

GRENADA
Dates from 1974 and features a nutmeg, a spice that is the main export of the island.

ST. KITTS & NEVIS
Designed in 1983. The colors stand for fertility, liberation, and African heritage.

SOUTH AMERICA

BRAZIL
Four new stars were added to the blue disk in 1992. These represent four new federal states.

ARGENTINA
Adopted in May 1810 to mark independence from Spain. The "Sun of May" was added in 1818.

PERU
The red and white colors were arranged into three stripes by Simón Bolívar in 1825.

COLOMBIA
Yellow, blue, and red are called the colors of Miranda after the Venezuelan rebel.

BOLIVIA
Dates from 1851. Red is for courage, green for the fertile land, and yellow for rich natural resources.

VENEZUELA
The colors of the rebel Miranda. The stars represent the provinces that joined the fight against Spain.

CHILE
Inspired by the Stars and Stripes, this flag dates from 1817. The star is to guide Chile to an honorable future.

PARAGUAY
The "Star of May" dates from May 1811 when Spanish rule was rejected. The arms were added in 1842.

ECUADOR
Has the same origin as the Colombian flag. Adopted in 1900. Colors symbolize the fight for freedom.

GUYANA
Adopted for independence in 1966. The flag is nicknamed "The Golden Arrow."

URUGUAY
Based on the Argentinian flag. But the stripes are like the U.S. Stars and Stripes.

SURINAME
Adopted in 1975 after independence. It is a mixture of the colors of the local political parties.

FLAGS OF EUROPE

Many European flags are hundreds of years old. The Swiss flag, for example, was first used by one of the Swiss cantons (regions) in 1291. Many of the flags are also religious or heraldic in origin. The Swedish flag combines both elements with colors derived from the national arms and a design based on a Christian cross.

European flags often use the Christian symbol of the cross. Denmark, Finland, Sweden, Norway, and Iceland all use a cross called the Scandinavian cross. It was first used by Denmark.

Crosses are also used on the flags of Greece and Britain. The British flag, called the Union Jack, is made up of three overlapping crosses. In 1606 the crosses of Scotland and England were combined to make the first "Union Flag." In 1801, the Irish cross of St. Patrick was added.

The French *tricolore* is one of the most famous flags. It was adopted as a symbol of liberty during the French Revolution in 1789. A tricolor design consists of three stripes of different colors. Other countries used this as a basis for flag designs to show their sympathy with the aims of the French Revolution.

In Eastern Europe, several flags use the pan-Slav colors of red, white, and blue.

These are based on the Russian flag. The flags of Slovenia and Slovakia are exactly like the Russian flag, but heraldic shields have been added so that people can tell the flags apart.

FRANCE
First used in this form in 1794. The *tricolore* (three colors) has inspired many flag designers around the world.

SPAIN
This version dates from 1785. For official occasions the flag has a coat of arms.

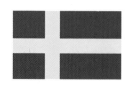

SWEDEN
Dates from the early 16th century. It has the Scandinavian cross first used by Denmark.

Map labels:
ICELAND
Norwegian Sea
SWEDEN
FINLAND
Gulf of Bothnia
North Sea
NORWAY
RUSSIA
Baltic Sea
BELGIUM
NETHERLANDS
DENMARK
CZECH REPUBLIC
IRELAND
UNITED KINGDOM
POLAND
SLOVAKIA
GERMANY
HUNGARY
LUXEMBOURG
ATLANTIC OCEAN
LIECHTENSTEIN
SLOVENIA
FRANCE
AUSTRIA
CROATIA
SWITZERLAND
ITALY
ROMANIA
PORTUGAL
BOSNIA AND HERZEGOVINA
SPAIN
MONACO
BULGARIA
ANDORRA
SAN MARINO
YUGOSLAVIA
VATICAN CITY
MACEDONIA
GREECE
Mediterranean Sea
ALBANIA
MALTA
CYPRUS

GERMANY
East and West Germany reunited in 1990. They kept the flag of West Germany, first used in 1818.

FINLAND
Dates from 1918. The colors represent lakes and snow. The design of the cross is based on the Danish flag.

NORWAY
Dates from 1821. It is the Danish flag with an extra blue cross. It became the national flag in 1899.

POLAND
The Polish coat of arms shows a white eagle on a red shield. Since 1919 the flag has used the same colors.

ITALY
The Italian tricolor is a direct copy of the French flag. It was adopted in the time of Napoleon.

YUGOSLAVIA
The blue-white-red tricolor was adopted in 1918. It is used by the new Yugoslavia, formed in 1992.

ENGLAND

SCOTLAND

UNITED KINGDOM
A combination of crosses representing England, Scotland, and Ireland. This form of the flag dates from 1801.

NORTHERN IRELAND

WALES

MACEDONIA
The flag was adopted in 1995. Greece disputed the original choice, the "Star of Vergina" on a red background.

ROMANIA
This combines the colors of the two provinces that united to form Romania in the 19th century.

GREECE
The nine stripes are said to stand for the nine syllables in the Greek motto meaning "Liberty or Death!"

BULGARIA
Dates from 1878. Like the Russian flag, but the blue stripe has been changed to green.

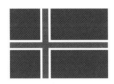

ICELAND
Dates from 1915. Exactly the same as the Norwegian flag, but the colors are reversed.

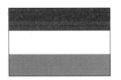

HUNGARY
Red, white, and green are the traditional colors of Hungary. This version of the flag dates from 1848.

PORTUGAL
The flag dates from 1911. The navigator's sphere indicates Portugal's achievements in world exploration.

AUSTRIA
The red-white-red flag dates back to the 12th century. The flag in this form became the national flag in 1918.

CZECH REPUBLIC
Slovakia separated from the Czech Republic in 1992. The Czech Republic kept the joint flag, used since 1920.

IRELAND
Based on the French *tricolore*. It dates from 1848 and became the national flag in 1919.

CROATIA
The colors were adopted in 1848. The small shields represent areas of land claimed by Croatia.

BOSNIA AND HERZEGOVINA
The flag was adopted in 1992. It uses the shield of a medieval king of Bosnia.

SLOVAKIA
A copy of the Russian flag. The coat of arms take their colors from the flag, not the other way around.

DENMARK
One of the oldest national flags. It has influenced the designs of the other Scandinavian flags.

NETHERLANDS
Originated with the supporters of William of Orange. An orange band was changed to red in the 17th century.

SWITZERLAND
The white cross on a red background is the traditional badge of the Swiss cantons. This form dates from 1814.

BELGIUM
Black, red, and yellow are traditional Belgian colors. This form dates from 1831.

ALBANIA
A double-headed eagle is the national symbol of Albania. A yellow star was added in 1946 and removed in 1992.

SLOVENIA
The flag uses the traditional Slovenian colors. Part of the coat of arms relates to the communist era.

CYPRUS
Adopted in 1960 after independence from Britain. The white background signifies peace.

LUXEMBOURG
The blue stripe was made paler at the end of the 19th century to make it different from the Dutch flag.

ANDORRA
Combines the colors of France and Spain. Identical to the Romanian flag except for the coat of arms.

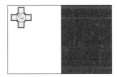

MALTA
These are the colors of the Knights of St. John who once ruled the island. The medal is the George Cross.

LIECHTENSTEIN
The red and blue of Liechtenstein date back to the 19th century. The coronet was added in 1937.

SAN MARINO
San Marino is the smallest republic in the world. The flag colors are taken from the San Marino coat of arms.

MONACO
The colors are those of the ruling Grimaldi family. The flag in this form dates from 1881.

VATICAN CITY
Adopted in 1929. The gold and silver keys of St. Peter are used as the emblem.

FLAGS OF AFRICA

The colors of the Ethiopian flag—green, red, and yellow—are the colors of the Rastafarian religion. Rastafarians believe that Emperor Haile Selassie of Ethiopia was the incarnation of God. These colors are used by several African countries in their flags. They are also known as the pan-African colors. Other parts of Africa have been influenced by the Arab world. The pan-Arab colors of black, green, red, and white are used in the flag of Sudan. After independence, many states adopted flags in the colors of their most powerful political parties.

Mediterranean Sea

TUNISIA
MOROCCO
ALGERIA
LIBYA
EGYPT
ERITREA
DJIBOUTI
CAPE VERDE
MAURITANIA
MALI
NIGER
CHAD
SUDAN
SENEGAL
GAMBIA
BURKINA FASO
GUINEA
GUINEA-BISSAU
NIGERIA
ETHIOPIA
SOMALIA
SIERRA LEONE
CENTRAL AFRICAN REPUBLIC
LIBERIA
GHANA
BENIN
CAMEROON
UGANDA
COTE D'IVOIRE
TOGO
KENYA
SAO TOME AND PRINCIPE
GABON
DEMOCRATIC REPUBLIC OF THE CONGO
RWANDA
EQUATORIAL GUINEA
BURUNDI
CONGO
TANZANIA
MALAWI
SEYCHELLES
ATLANTIC OCEAN
ANGOLA
ZAMBIA
COMOROS
MADAGASCAR
MOZAMBIQUE
MAURITIUS
NAMIBIA
ZIMBABWE
BOTSWANA
INDIAN OCEAN
SWAZILAND
LESOTHO
SOUTH AFRICA
Cape of Good Hope
Red Sea

SUDAN
Adopted in 1970. The pan-Arab colors replaced the flag used since independence in 1956.

ALGERIA
Originally the flag of the liberation movement. Officially adopted on independence in 1962.

DEM. REP. OF THE CONGO
First used in 1960 when the Belgian Congo became independent, it was readopted in 1997.

LIBYA
Introduced in 1977. This is the only flag that uses one plain color. Green is the color of Islam.

CHAD
Similar to Romania's flag. It is another combination of French and pan-African colors.

NIGER
Adopted in 1959, a year before independence. The disk in the center represents the sun.

ANGOLA
Based on the flag of the left-wing party (the MPLA), which won a civil war in the 1970s.

MALI
Adopted in 1960. The pan-African colors make this a mirror-image of Guinea's flag.

SOUTH AFRICA
This flag was first raised on April 27, 1994. It marked the end of white minority rule in South Africa.

MAURITANIA
Adopted in 1958. The color and symbols express the Islamic foundations of this country.

EGYPT
Dates from 1984. The emblem is the eagle of Saladin, who was a famous Muslim ruler.

TANZANIA
Combines the colors of Tanganyika and Zanzibar, which formed a union in 1964.

NIGERIA
Adopted in 1960 on independence from Britain. The design symbolizes the green land and Niger river.

ETHIOPIA
The colors of the stripes inspired the pan-African and Rastafarian colors. The star, introduced in 1996, symbolizes national unity.

NAMIBIA
Adopted on independence in 1990. Uses the colors, but not the design, of the liberation party's flag.

MOZAMBIQUE
Based on the flag of the freedom fighters. This version was introduced in 1983 and replaced an earlier design.

ZAMBIA
Adopted in 1964 and based on the colors of the first ruling party.

SOMALIA
Adopted in 1960. Based on the United Nations flag as Somalia was a UN territory before independence.

CENTRAL AFRICAN REPUBLIC
Adopted in 1958. A combination of the French *tricolore* and the pan-African colors.

BOTSWANA
Adopted in 1966 on independence. The blue background stands for the importance of rain to this dry country.

MADAGASCAR
Introduced in 1958. Red and white represent the Merina people, green is for the coastal people.

KENYA
Adopted in 1963. Based on the flag of the main political party—the Kenya African National Union.

CAMEROON
This version dates from 1975. Features the pan-African colors of red, green, and yellow.

MOROCCO
Originally plain red. The green star, sometimes called Solomon's Seal, was added in 1915.

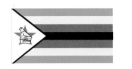

ZIMBABWE
Introduced in 1980. Based on the colors of the main liberation party. Includes the national bird.

CONGO
Introduced in 1959. Not used while the communists were in power, but has been used since 1991.

COTE D'IVOIRE
Adopted in 1959, a year before independence. The colors stand for the dry north and the green southern forests.

BURKINA FASO
Adopted in 1984. Red, green, and yellow are the pan-African colors.

GABON
Adopted in 1960 on independence from France. The colors represent the forests, the sun, and the sea.

GUINEA
Introduced in 1958. The arrangement of the pan-African colors is like the French *tricolore*.

GHANA
Introduced in 1957. It was the first modern African flag and inspired many other countries' flags.

UGANDA
Based on the colors of a political party. The national symbol, a crested crane, is in the middle.

ERITREA
One of the newest national flags. Eritrea became independent from Ethiopia in 1993.

SENEGAL
A green star was added in the early 1960s to avoid confusion with Mali's flag.

TUNISIA
Based on the Turkish flag. It dates from about 1835, making it the oldest African flag used continuously.

MALAWI
Adopted on independence in 1964. Based on the Malawi Congress Party flag.

BENIN
Pan-African colors adopted in 1959. A communist-style flag was used between 1975 and 1990.

LIBERIA
Closely modeled on the U.S. flag. Liberia was colonized by African Americans in the 1840s.

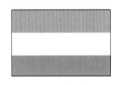

SIERRA LEONE
Adopted on independence in 1961. This was the winning design in a competition.

TOGO
Adopted in 1960. Another flag in the pan-African colors. The white star stands for national independence.

GUINEA-BISSAU
Adopted in 1974 on independence from Portugal. Based on the leading political party's flag.

LESOTHO
Adopted in 1987. This design replaced the flag used since independence in 1966.

EQUATORIAL GUINEA
Adopted on independence in 1968. Central emblem changed between 1972 and 1979.

BURUNDI
Adopted in 1962. The central emblem was altered in 1967. The stars stand for unity, work, and progress.

RWANDA
The letter "R" was added to the flag in 1962 to avoid confusion with Guinea's flag.

DJIBOUTI
Adopted in 1977 on independence from France. Based on the flag of the freedom-fighters.

SWAZILAND
Adopted on independence in 1968. Like Kenya's flag, this features an African shield.

GAMBIA
Adopted in 1965 on independence from Britain. The blue stripe stands for the Gambia River.

CAPE VERDE
Introduced in 1992. Replaced a pan-African flag. The ten stars represent the ten islands of Cape Verde.

COMOROS
This version was introduced in 1996. It features Islamic green and a star for each island.

MAURITIUS
Adopted on independence in 1968. The four colors are found in the island's coat of arms.

SAO TOME AND PRINCIPE
Introduced on independence in 1975. Based on the liberation movement's flag.

SEYCHELLES
Adopted in 1996. Blue is for the sky and sea, yellow for the sun, red symbolizes the people, white is for justice, and green depicts the land.

FLAGS OF THE FORMER SOVIET UNION REPUBLICS AND THE MIDDLE EAST

The Union of Soviet Socialist Republics (USSR) split into 15 independent countries. The former USSR used the famous communist Red Flag, which featured the hammer and sickle emblem together with the yellow outline star.

Russia, or the Russian Federation, is still the largest country in the area. Russia now uses its ancient tricolor flag. This white, blue, and red flag has been copied by many countries, including Slovenia and Slovakia. These colors are sometimes called the pan-Slav colors.

Some of the countries have gone back to flags they used at the end of World War I, just before the USSR was formed.

The Middle East is the home of Islam, a religion founded in what is now Saudia Arabia in the 7th century. The traditional color of Islam is green and the Islamic emblem is the crescent and star. Turkey was the first country to use the crescent and star on its flag.

Many flags in the Middle East use the pan-Arab colors of red, white, black, and green. The words *Allahu Akbar*, which mean "God is Great," are used on the flags of several countries including Afghanistan and Iran.

RUSSIA
Introduced by Peter the Great in 1700. It was not used during the communist period (1917-91).

KAZAKSTAN
Designed in 1992. It features the sun and a soaring eagle. There is a traditional Kazak design on the hoist.

SAUDI ARABIA
The words are the Islamic creed: "There is no God but Allah, and Muhammad is the Prophet of Allah."

IRAN
Adopted in 1980. The lettering says *Allahu Akbar* ("God is Great") 22 times. The emblem is a sword and crescents.

TURKEY
The first national flag to use the crescent and star symbols. This has inspired many others countries.

UKRAINE
Dates from 1848. It was also used between 1918 and 1920, but was not used again until 1991.

YEMEN
Introduced when North and South Yemen were united in 1990. It combines elements from both the original flags.

TURKMENISTAN
Introduced in 1992. The design in the hoist is a carpet, the most famous local product.

IRAQ
The basic form dates from 1963. During the Gulf War the words *Allahu Akbar* were added.

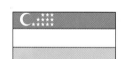

UZBEKISTAN
Dates from 1991. The moon stands for rebirth and the stars for the importance of astrology and astronomy.

OMAN
Originally plain red. The emblem and the white and green panels were added in 1970.

BELARUS
Adopted in 1995 following independence from the former Soviet Union. Red stands for its communist history and green for its vegetation.

KYRGYZSTAN
Adopted in 1992 after the collapse of communism. The central emblem is a traditional Kyrgyzstani tent.

SYRIA
Originally the flag of the United Arab Republic. It was first used by Syria in 1980.

TAJIKISTAN
Adopted in 1992. Tajikistan has ethnic links with Iran and the flags use the same colors.

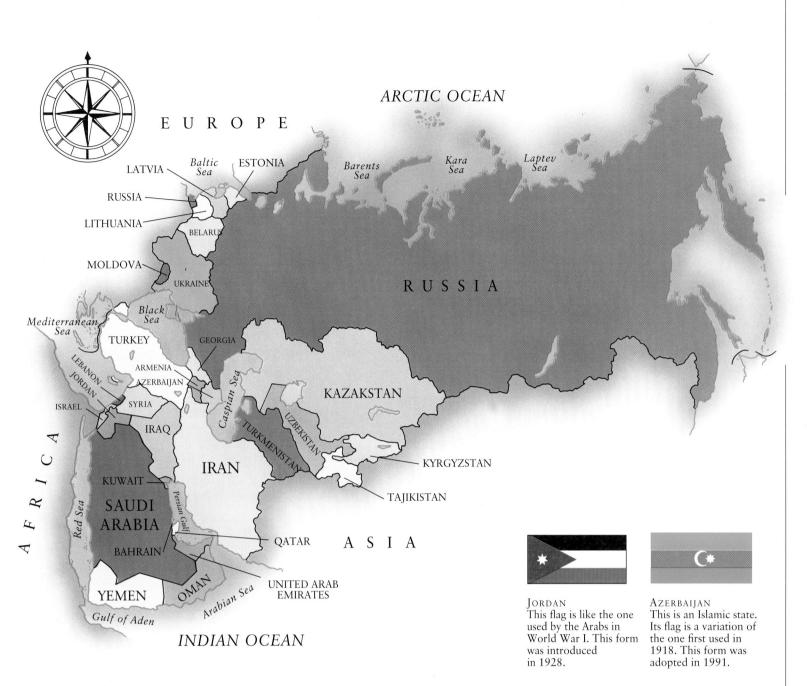

ARCTIC OCEAN

E U R O P E

Baltic Sea
LATVIA
ESTONIA
Barents Sea
Kara Sea
Laptev Sea

RUSSIA
LITHUANIA
BELARUS

MOLDOVA
UKRAINE

R U S S I A

Black Sea

Mediterranean Sea

TURKEY
GEORGIA
ARMENIA
AZERBAIJAN
SYRIA
IRAQ
IRAN

Caspian Sea

KAZAKSTAN

UZBEKISTAN
TURKMENISTAN

KYRGYZSTAN

TAJIKISTAN

A F R I C A

LEBANON
JORDAN
ISRAEL

Red Sea

KUWAIT
SAUDI ARABIA
BAHRAIN

Persian Gulf

QATAR

A S I A

UNITED ARAB EMIRATES

YEMEN
OMAN
Arabian Sea

Gulf of Aden

INDIAN OCEAN

JORDAN
This flag is like the one used by the Arabs in World War I. This form was introduced in 1928.

AZERBAIJAN
This is an Islamic state. Its flag is a variation of the one first used in 1918. This form was adopted in 1991.

UNITED ARAB EMIRATES
Also in the pan-Arab colors. Introduced in 1971 when the seven emirates were united.

GEORGIA
This flag in cherry red, black, and white, was designed in 1917 and revived in 1990.

LITHUANIA
Adopted in 1918. It was suppressed during the communist period and was restored in 1988.

LATVIA
Adopted in 1917. It was restored in 1990 after the collapse of communism.

ESTONIA
Introduced in 1881 and became the national flag in 1920. Not used during the communist period.

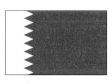

MOLDOVA
Moldova was once a part of Romania and their flags are very similar except for the Moldovan coat of arms.

ARMENIA
The flag was first used in 1918 and was revived in 1990. The design represents a rainbow over Mount Ararat.

ISRAEL
Introduced in 1948. The emblem is the Star of David. White and blue are traditional colors in Judaism.

KUWAIT
A flag in the pan-Arab colors of red, white, green, and black. Introduced in 1961.

QATAR
Originally white and plain red. Over the years the red has changed to a maroon color.

LEBANON
The tree in the center is the famous cedar of Lebanon. The flag was first hoisted in 1943.

BAHRAIN
Very like the flag of Qatar. At one time, all the Persian Gulf states had similar flags to this one.

FLAGS OF ASIA

World War II ended in 1945. At that time many Asian countries were still ruled by foreign powers. Since then, most countries in the region have become independent and govern themselves. The first country in this part of the world to gain independence after the war was the Philippines, which became independent of the United States in 1946.

The newly independent countries were free to design their own flags. The flag of Burma features a rice plant, which is a very important crop in Asia. Pakistan chose an Islamic green flag but added a white stripe to symbolize tolerance of other religions.

Communism became a powerful force in Asia in the 1940s and the communists took over in China in 1949. The Chinese flag is based on the Red Flag from the former USSR. Red and yellow are the traditional Chinese colors as well as being the colors of communism.

China, Laos, North Korea, and Vietnam are still communist countries. Mongolia, one of the very first communist states, has recently introduced some reforms and removed the yellow star of socialism from its flag in 1992.

Japan has always been an independent country and the red sun disk on the flag dates back over 600 years, although it only became part of the national flag in 1870.

CHINA
Introduced in 1949 and deliberately based on the Red Flag of the former USSR.

INDIA
Adopted in 1947 just before independence. The central image is a Buddhist wheel of life dating back 2,000 years.

INDONESIA
This was chosen as the national flag in 1949 when Indonesia gained independence from the Netherlands.

MONGOLIA
There used to be a yellow star above the emblem. The emblem stands for a whole host of different things including friendship.

PAKISTAN
Based on the flag of the Muslim League. This League led the fight for independence in the 1940s.

MYANMAR
Adopted on independence in 1948. The emblem was changed to a rice plant and cog wheel in 1974.

AFGHANISTAN
Introduced in 1992. The emblem includes elements from earlier versions of the arms, as well as religious inscriptions.

THAILAND
Adopted in 1917. The blue stripe was added that year to show support for the Allies in World War I.

JAPAN
The central red disk of the sun represents sincerity and passion, the white background purity and honesty.

MALAYSIA
Three stripes, standing for three new states, were added in 1963 when Malaya became Malaysia.

VIETNAM
Adopted in 1945. Used by North Vietnam during the civil war. In 1975 it was used again for the whole country.

PHILIPPINES
Designed in 1898 by revolutionaries who wanted to overthrow the Spanish rulers. Adopted in 1946.

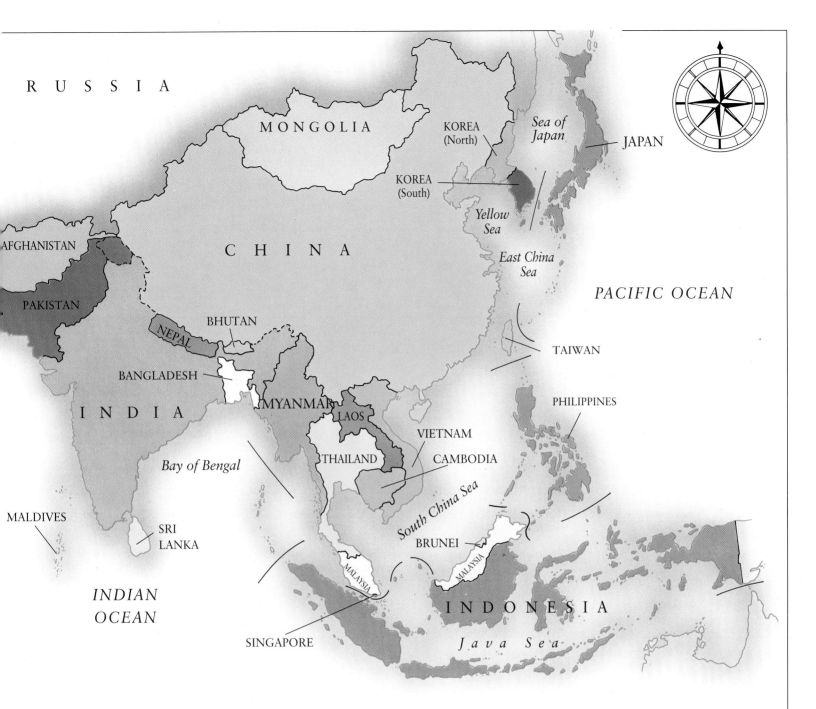

R U S S I A

M O N G O L I A

KOREA (North)

Sea of Japan

JAPAN

KOREA (South)

C H I N A

Yellow Sea

East China Sea

PACIFIC OCEAN

AFGHANISTAN

PAKISTAN

BHUTAN

NEPAL

BANGLADESH

I N D I A

MYANMAR

LAOS

VIETNAM

THAILAND

CAMBODIA

TAIWAN

PHILIPPINES

Bay of Bengal

MALDIVES

SRI LANKA

South China Sea

BRUNEI

MALAYSIA

MALAYSIA

INDIAN OCEAN

I N D O N E S I A

Java Sea

SINGAPORE

LAOS
Adopted in 1975. Originally the flag of the communist group, the Lao Patriotic Front. The white full moon stands for the future.

CAMBODIA
Three towers of the famous temple of Angkor Wat feature on this flag which was readopted in 1993.

BANGLADESH
Introduced in 1971 when Bangladesh became independent of Pakistan. The red disk is the "sun of freedom."

NEPAL
The only national flag that is not a rectangle. The white shapes represent the sun and moon.

NORTH KOREA
Adopted in 1948. The red star is a symbol of communism and represents the Korean Workers' Party.

SOUTH KOREA
Based on an old flag from before Japan's occupation in 1910. The white background is for peace.

SRI LANKA
Adopted in 1948 when Ceylon, as it was called, became independent. Green and orange panels were added in 1951.

BHUTAN
Updated in 1965. The wingless dragon is the national symbol. *Bhutan* means "Land of the Thunder Dragon."

TAIWAN
The island of Taiwan kept the Chinese national flag when the mainland became communist in 1949.

SINGAPORE
Adopted in 1959. The five stars stand for five ideals: democracy, peace, progress, justice, and equality.

BRUNEI
Originally plain yellow. The black-and-white stripe was introduced in 1906 and the arms added in 1959.

MALDIVES
Adopted in 1965 on independence from Britain. The green rectangle and the crescent show the influence of Islam.

GLOSSARY

ARMORIAL
Having to do with heraldry or heraldic coats of arms.

BADGE
An emblem used by a person or institution which can be used separately or put onto a flag. A heraldic badge is given out by the head of the family and used in addition to the family coat of arms.

BADGE FLAG
A flag using a heraldic badge. A badge flag could be used by a knight's servants and followers but only the knight could fly his own banner or standard.

BANNER
An armorial banner is a heraldic flag which reproduces the color and pattern of the shield from a coat of arms.

BUNTING
The name for the material traditionally used to make flags. Decorative strings of flags are also called bunting.

CANTON
The name for the upper hoist quarter of a flag. That is, if a flag is divided into quarters, the top quarter nearest the flagpole. The second quarter, farthest from the pole, is called the upper fly canton. The third quarter is called the lower hoist canton and the fourth quarter, the lower fly canton.

CIVIL ENSIGN
The form of a national flag used at sea by merchant and private ships.

CIVIL FLAG
The form of a national flag used on land by private persons and institutions.

COLORS
The flags used by units of the armed forces, often decorated with details of battles won.

COMMISSION PENNANT
A long, tapering flag used by a warship to show it is operational.

COURTESY ENSIGN
The flag hoisted by ships visiting a foreign port as a courtesy, or politeness, to the host country. A courtesy ensign is usually the civil ensign of the host country.

EMBLEM
A symbol or heraldic device representing an individual, country, or organization.

ENSIGN
The flag denoting nationality used by ships of all kinds. In some armed forces the title of the most junior rank of officer was "ensign" because traditionally it was his job to carry the flag.

FIELD
The background or basic color of a flag or coat of arms.

FIMBRIATION
A narrow border of color between two colors on a flag.

FINIAL
The ornamental shape at the top of a flagstaff. Finials are most often found on indoor or parade flags.

FLAG OF CONVENIENCE
The civil ensign of a country where a foreign ship is registered because rules and standards are less strict than elsewhere.

FLY
The part of a flag away from the hoist. This may also be called the "flying end."

GUIDON
A flag which led or guided troops, usually featuring the livery colors and badge of the leader.

HALYARDS
The ropes on a mast or pole to which flags are attached for hoisting.

HEADING
A tube of material attached to the hoist edge of a flag and containing the hoist rope or fitted with other means of attaching the flag to the halyards. Also known as a sleeve.

HOIST
The part of a flag nearest the flagpole.

HOIST ROPE
A rope sewn into the heading or sleeve of a flag and used to attach it to the halyards.

JOLLY ROGER
The usual name for the flag flown by pirates. The black flag, often with a Skull and Crossbones, meant that no mercy would be shown.

LIVERY COLORS
The two main colors used in a coat of arms or a set of other traditional colors. These colors were then used in the clothes given or "delivered" to retainers to show whose servants they were.

MERCHANT FLAG
An older name for the civil ensign.

MORSE CODE
A way of sending messages using short signals (dots) and long signals (dashes). A flag can be used to send messages in Morse code. The flag is held upright for a dot and sideways for a dash.

MOTTO
A few words, or a saying, often put at the bottom of a coat of arms, which sum up the aims or ideals of the individual, organization, or country to whom the coat of arms belongs.

NATIONAL FLAG
The ordinary flag used to show nationality.

NAVAL ENSIGN
The form of national flag used by warships.

OBVERSE
The "front" of the flag as seen with the flagstaff on the observer's left.

PENNANT
A triangular flag of any length. Pennants are sometimes used as souvenirs.

PENNON
A triangular or swallow-tailed flag usually carried on a lance.

REVERSE
The "back" of the flag as seen with the flagstaff on the observer's right.

SALTIRE
A diagonal cross, as in the Scottish flag.

SCANDINAVIAN CROSS
A cross with one arm longer than the other as seen in the flag of Denmark.

SCHWENKEL
An extended strip of fabric added along the top of a flag.

SEMAPHORE
A signaling system using two flags with a sign for each letter of the alphabet.

SIGNAL FLAGS
Any kind of flag or flags used to send messages or information.

SLEEVE
A tube of fabric attached to the hoist edge of the flag and through which the stave is passed. Also called a heading.

STANDARD
A standard is any important flag or vexilloid. The flag of an important individual may also be called a standard.

STATE FLAG
The form of the national flag used by the government or for official purposes.

STAVE
The wooden pole used to carry an indoor or parade flag.

SUPPORTERS
In heraldry, supporters are the figures or animals (called beasts) which hold up, or support, the shield of a coat of arms. They are placed on either side of the shield.

SWALLOW-TAIL FLAG
A flag which has had a triangle of material cut from the flying end so it looks like the forked tail of the bird called a swallow.

TRICOLOR
A flag with three vertical or horizontal stripes of different colors.

VEXILLOID
An object on a pole, used in earlier times as flags are used today.

VEXILLOLOGY
The scientific and systematic study of flags and related emblems.

VEXILLUM
The free-flying fabric decoration which was added to vexilloids around 2,000 years ago and which were the forerunners of modern fabric flags.

INDEX